Pragmatic Wisdom Vol. 6

Stoic Lessons on Thinking Well

James Bellerjeau

A Fine Idea

Contents

Chapter One

Why Do Anything?
An Introduction to
the Stoic Lessons

D ear friends. Join me on a journey to discover what it means to live a good life. Our inspiration in this quest is Seneca's Moral Letters to Lucilius, revisited and revised for our modern times. The search for what it means to live a good life was not new in Seneca's day, and it will not be old when we are all long gone.

Although these are not Seneca's letters, they honor both his wisdom and his instructions for new students. That is, we should grapple with deep thoughts and make our understanding of the truth personal.

Because no one has a monopoly on the truth, we can each contribute to the puzzle. **The reason to do anything is to answer a question that has not been answered, or at a minimum to answer it for yourself.**

In answering life's deepest questions, would it not be foolish for us to pass by the foundational stones laid by the great thinkers who labored before us? Seneca himself in search of inspiration says in his Letter 2:

> I am wont to cross over even into the enemy's camp, — not as a deserter, but as a scout.

Let us all be avid scouts of the great thinkers, seeking out their every camp with the mindset of anthropologists unearthing meaning from among the ruins. Although Seneca's words have been mined by many for centuries, each generation keeps turning up gemstones.

Thus, with this series of Pragmatic Wisdom for Busy People, let us polish old stones to show them in a new light, and in washing off the mud and debris, reveal what fresh reflections may appear.

Be well.

PS — You can read each of the volumes independently, as it suits your time and your interests. Dedicated readers will find, however, that their understanding of each volume will increase upon reading further volumes. The sincere student may therefore wish to have the full set of Stoic letters: Pragmatic Wisdom for the Sincere Student.

Chapter Two

On Anxiety

There are more things apt to worry us than there are to wound us; but we're harmed in our heads more than by anyone else's hand

I know you are ready for learning because you have already taken one of life's main lessons to heart.

Fall seven times and stand up eight

So goes the Japanese proverb, and so also go the lives of the fortunate. It is our fate to fall, and only when it happens do we know how quickly we'll rise to our feet again.

You may think you are a trooper, able to withstand whatever fate throws at you. Think how reassuring it is to have your faith tested and come out judged a success.

The pandemic closed your workplace, cut you off from your friends, and kept you a prisoner in your house. Everything you didn't realize you took for granted was whisked away without notice, and in the stillness that remained you noticed that you remained.

Be thankful that you have been subjected to tests that you would never choose to submit to and come out victorious! This shows strength of character more than any course of study alone.

There are more things, dear reader, apt to worry us than there are to wound us; but we're harmed in our heads more than by anyone else's hand.

I know you will recall my prior teachings, that whatever happens to us is not unwanted if we are sufficient in ourselves. This is no doubt true, though I am writing here to advise you to be kinder to yourself.

Troubles will come to you without you wishing them, so don't trouble yourself before they do. The specters that disturb your dreams may slink by unseen, and in any event, they are not today knocking at your door.

Anxiety comes in four flavors:

- being bothered by things that are behind us,

- being bothered by things that should be beneath our notice,

- being bothered before any trouble is brewing, and

- being bothered by things that are no bane at all.

We agonize ourselves more thoroughly than a medieval torturer in the dungeons of our minds when we relive painful moments in our pasts over and over.

We also blow things out of proportion, dream disasters, and jump at shadows. Offense can be found any place one looks, if one goes looking for it. Those who have experienced real hardship are less likely to be troubled by trifles.

But let's leave aside differences of opinion about who is harmed the most by the least and focus on the remaining two anxieties: Worry about that which has not happened yet, and worry about that which should not worry you at all.

Everywhere you look, disaster looms. Social media, television talking heads, and politicians all proclaim: The heat death of the planet from man-made global warming is overdue, although you may be carried off by floodwaters before you can be burned alive.

Rogue regimes threaten our way of life, if not our very lives, be it Iran or North Korea, Russia, Venezuela, or the Middle East. Our livelihoods are under attack from afar by China, and closer to home our border with Mexico groans with South American immigrants.

Before you give in to existential despair, ask yourself this: "Does any of this affect what I am doing today, and am I any worse off in a tangible way? Or do I accept the prophesy of doom without any evidence that I am actually damned?"

If you wonder how to tell whether the trouble is real or imagined, you can use this rule of thumb: You are either affected right now or will be afflicted tomorrow, or both.

The right now is within your purview to assess and do not let another tell you that you suffer when plainly you do not. We will come to tomorrow soon enough, so first acknowledge that today is OK.

"But" you say, "tomorrow may be terrible if we don't act to prevent catastrophe now." I urge you to remember that history is heaped more with gloomy predictions that never came to pass than those accurately foretold.

The forests are dying, the oil is running out, the air is becoming unbreathable, crime waves will destroy cities. I do not say that bad things do not happen, oh no, but that prophesies of bad things are no good guide for what they will be or when they will arrive.

Some people take a thrill in being terrified. The more dire the outlook, the happier they are to hear of our terrible fortune.

But my dear reader, it is a mistake to take the media's frenzy for anything other than whipping up the masses for profit. Too many uncritically accept all that is critical without questioning the track record of the purveyors of doom.

Who dares question the "consensus" opinion when the fate awaiting "deniers" is not in doubt: Ostracism, if not exile? That the consensus may be based on little more than opinion itself matters not when its breathless repetition blows it into a castle in the sky.

When you remember that most prophesies of disaster do not come to pass, you make room for yourself to be happy today. Even if you will suffer later, you do not suffer now, so why do you make yourself sad with the anticipation of your sorrows?

If you wish, you could bask yourself entirely in worries, but what sort of existence would that be? Better to be a hopeless optimist than a hopeless pessimist. You are just as likely to have your comforting daydreams come to pass as your nightmares, for all the good that dwelling on either will do you.

Thus, consider bright thoughts alongside dour ones, and when unsure which will come to pass, pick the one that makes you feel better.

Even if you think the hill slopes downward, point yourself upwards, because you do not need to add your own momentum to its direction. Rather than letting yourself be carried along with the weeping crowd, take a single step to the side and orient yourself to the sun.

I commend this course to you lightly, because it is a slight solution. Let the next person say "I wish for the best."

You are infinitely firmer in your foundation by virtue of embracing the view "Let come what may. I am made stronger by my fortune because my reaction to my circumstance is more important than my current situation."

But I know I browbeat you without need, for you are beating your own path in the right direction.

To finish today, I will address a proclamation of supposed wisdom for you. Consider the saying

Time you enjoy wasting is not wasted time

from Marthe Troly-Curtin. Lest you get overly fond of this thought, my dear reader, for it is surely appealing, remember that just as a great wall is built a single brick at a time, so too was Rome dismantled. Our lives are spent in building up or in breaking down, and we must choose a direction.

Or if you prefer to stay with the world of rock and roll, I cannot say it better than those latter-day philosophers Pink Floyd:

Ticking away the moments that make up a dull
day
You fritter and waste the hours in an offhand way
Kicking around on a piece of ground in your
home town
Waiting for someone or something to show you
the way
Tired of lying in the sunshine, staying home to
watch the rain
You are young and life is long, and there is time
to kill today
And then, one day you find, ten years have got
behind you
No one told you when to run, you missed the
starting gun

I know that you will not mind partaking in the font of
wisdom wherever it may bubble up. For it is not the vessel that
determines the value of a drink, but the contents themselves.

Be well.

Chapter Three

On Consistency

The way to identify a wise person is to observe the one who maintains consistency in the face of passions all around them

To be healthy, to be of sound mind and body, and to be facing a voluntary decision to call a halt to your current pursuits. I am happy for you, and as much for myself, if I have helped you arrive at this point of self-reflection.

I caution you, dear reader, that you cannot be a hypocrite. It is not enough to think good thoughts; you must transform thoughts into deeds. The lessons of philosophy are hard-won, and their proof is in the pudding.

Though you think your thoughts are pure, if your actions are compromised, your lessons will have availed you little.

- Consider the coach who exhorts the team: do as I *say*, not as I *do*. From what authority does he speak, and why should we listen?

- Consider the political party that uses every leverage

and maneuver when it has the reins of power but bitterly decries their use by the other party when the electoral winds have shifted.

Why do we give such hypocrites a moment's consideration?

Knowing the nature of humankind, and how easily the weak can become the powerful, the drafters of the U.S. Constitution created many checks and balances on the unfettered exercises of power by a bare majority. We now see the guardrails recklessly dismantled in the raw pursuit of power.

None of our politicians doing the dirty work ask themselves why it was these limits were put in place, and what furies we unleash by their removal. We could forgive them for their folly, except that we are all fellow passengers in the bus they are steering ever closer towards the cliff's edge.

"Are you telling me to be a saint," you ask. "Am I never to place a wrong foot or risk being seen as a false student?"

I do not require that you be without fault, although indeed some are able to match every thought and deed. But nor can you be reckless. Credibility is built upon consistency.

Each time you say one thing and do another, you are a hypocrite. How many times can you wear this cloak if you expect others not to assume it is your habitual dress?

And particularly if you seek to hold others accountable for their sins while you sell yourself indulgences, don't be surprised if the bedrock of your beliefs is eroded.

Though all around you changes, you shall be consistent. Though all around you stays the same, if it goes against the proper wisdom you have learned, you shall be consistent.

Fads and trends come and go like wildfires burning through a dry landscape. They burn fiercely, whipped by great winds, threatening all whom fate has put in their path. But you know that the flames of fads burn out as quickly as they arise, with the difference being these flames burn only those who grasp them willingly.

- For many years it was business suits, suddenly khakis appeared, then came Patagonia vests, and now hoodies slouch into the boardroom.

- Pity the poor necktie, whose constricting embrace will grace no more necks. To chase fads is to lose consistency.

- Your closets will not groan with the weight of wardrobes you do not wear, for you will remember that your simple, durable clothing is functional, not ornamental.

You know I am fond of the Buddha, who has managed to capture great wisdom in a few words. I borrow today from his store, in the hopes of paying forward the debt:

> Even as a great rock is not shaken by the wind,
> the wise man is not shaken by praise or by
> blame.

The way to identify a wise person is to observe the one who maintains consistency in the face of passions all around them. What meaning does the praise of the masses bring? What lesson do you learn from the criticism of the ignorant?

You are as well served to assume that the croak of the crow is encouragement for your good deeds as you are to fear a seagull's droppings landing on your back are a warning.

What I am saying is this: Do not be tempted by sweet praise or pained by bitter criticism from anyone whose opinion and character you do not know and trust.

And as is my wont of late, I give you an additional gift to reinforce the notion I am trying to tease out:

> It is an invincible greatness of mind not to be elevated or dejected with good or ill fortune. A wise man is content with his lot, whatever it be — without wishing for what he has not.

You will recognize I dip once more into the deep well that is Seneca.

If you once learn to be happy with what you have and, as importantly, not sad about what you don't have, you will have arrived at a state of unassailable strength.

And once arriving at this peak, you will see that any step in another direction is inevitably a step downwards, making it easy to maintain your resolve.

Be well.

Chapter Four

On Finding Joy in the Right Places

Life is meant for living, and joy is a sign your life has found meaning, provided its source comes from within

Y ou may expect from others that they write of the latest celebrity romance making the rounds in Hollywood, or perhaps the latest politician "flamed" by a late-night comedian for being caught in another lie.

Perhaps they shall compare notes on the sports teams currently in season and describe who has chased after a ball most adroitly.

Not me, and not today. Instead, I write something of lasting value, that will accrue to your benefit as well as mine.

And what is this thing of "lasting value" I hold out before you? It is this simple advice: To seek joy in the right places.

You do this first by fostering a sound mind. A well-ordered mind is both the pre-condition for all your further philosophical progress, as well as the ultimate outcome.

When you are self-sufficient, you know that your satisfaction cannot come from strangers bearing gifts. Though you believe you are likely to always be on the receiving end of life's bounty — through a combination of your talents, your hard work, and your prior successes — nothing external is guaranteed.

Your happiness, dear reader, is your highest aim, and you aim best when you direct your gaze within. Learn to be happy with who you are, where you are, and what you have, and you have learned the recipe for joy.

"Am I not to take pleasure in anything the world has to offer? Why else have we been gifted with our various senses if not to savor a fine meal, linger over a lovely sunset, or dwell in the delight of well-played music?"

I do not counsel you to be a curmudgeon, taking pleasure only in denying others theirs. Nor should you take up the scourge of the ascetic.

Life is meant for living, and joy is a sign your life has found meaning, provided its source comes from within.

But do not mistake a passing pleasure for the joy that comes from deep reflection and a true understanding of where value is created. You enjoy eating, drinking, and dancing, and your heart is light. Joy is what remains when the things you enjoy are taken from you.

Finding joy in oneself will not happen by accident. It takes preparation, contemplation, and study.

The business of being happy is a serious business.

- Have you trained your mind to be content with nothing or little?

- Have you curbed your passions to the extent that the words of others arouse neither your praise nor your ire?

- Though your body fails you in innumerable ways, adding insult to injury, does your mind rise above to remind you that the body is just a vessel and the container is not the content?

It is true, dear reader, that if you enjoy only superficial pleasures, then you will suffer from superficial worries. But many a person has drowned themselves in a puddle of concerns a mile wide but only an inch deep.

If you can find space for deep thinking, you can create the conditions for uncovering deep joy.

If you do things for the right reasons, uncompelled by anyone and anything external, not needing luxuries or status or wealth for your happiness, then you are on the path of finding a wellspring of joy that will never cease flowing.

I return to Ralph Waldo Emerson to borrow from his fount of wisdom, for I know that his well cannot be run dry:

> To be yourself in a world that is constantly trying to make you something else is the greatest accomplishment.

The temptations of modern life are unavoidable, and so are the voices whispering to you that your happiness lies in their hands. If only you had this car, that handbag, those shoes, and a promotion, then you would be satisfied.

Never mind that in the time you spend longing, you are postponing living. And buying today's must-have items only puts you on the treadmill to be compelled to purchase tomorrow's.

The only thing you truly control is what you think. Thus, the path to happiness is not built upon pavers of enjoyment, but from choices: You must decide what you want and stick with your decisions. If you make well-considered decisions and are happy with your decisions, you will be on the way to lasting joy.

I will add two sayings to balance my accounts and tip the scales in my favor. They come courtesy of India and are proof that we need not look for glitters of gold to find treasure lying in plain view.

Guru Paramhansa Yogananda directs:

Learn to be calm and you will always be happy.

He speaks of the well-ordered mind that is the pre-condition for joy.

And the Buddha in his wisdom reminds us of what reward awaits us when we focus within:

When desires go, joy comes.

Though I myself do not desire to part from you, I take joy in knowing that you will come to understanding when my letter comes to you.

Be well.

Chapter Five

On Conquering Fear

I will tell you how to banish the demons that bedevil you

You commented that you are finding ways to find joy and not mere enjoyment, but that your mind is still troubled by the troubles that people too active in the world of business face.

- You are fighting frivolous lawsuits filed by unscrupulous lawyers, you must fend off unfounded accusations from claimants who would profit from your pain.

- You are at risk of shareholder lawsuits and regulatory investigations, and sanctions hang over your head like the Sword of Damocles.

It is a wonder to me that you find any tranquility at all when you allow this parade of demons to march through your thoughts unbidden!

The future is uncertain for all of us, dear reader. Why destroy your happiness today because it may come under attack tomorrow?

I will tell you how to banish the demons that bedevil you. Contemplate from the safety of your home the worst that may happen in each of your disaster scenarios, and how much those outcomes would trouble you.

Draw worries out of your mind like you would draw venom from the site of a poisonous snake's bite. Spit them out on paper so you can study them at your leisure where they cannot harm you.

The actual harm awaiting you is often not nearly as bad as the amount of anxiety you create in anticipation. Laugh at the myriad ways in which your mind seeks to burden you with cares.

The ultimate harm that can come to you is either not worth your bother, or it will be so serious that it will also end your life and with it your worries.

You know from what we have discussed earlier that the loss of power, prestige, or possessions should not discomfit you, for these are fair-weather friends and no basis for inner peace.

"But" you say, "what if I fear a lingering and gruesome death from cancer? What if I lose not my possessions, but my self-possession, in losing control of my faculties?"

In the first case, there is no such thing as the unendurable. You either endure or succumb. And anything you bear willingly you reduce the sting of suffering from.

If, however, you prove in the circumstance to be unwilling or unable, your fate is the same as countless others who have gone before you under every circumstance imaginable. In the great sweep of time, your and their suffering ends just the same.

In the second case, you either know your mind and your thoughts, in which case you are still their master, or you do not, in which case you are not there to bemoan their loss.

Your loved ones may suffer to see you thus incapacitated, but you do not suffer directly because another suffers. And keep in mind that if your loved ones would hear and honor your wishes, they would not suffer either in seeing your condition, for no one wishes their loved ones to suffer on their account.

The only proper occasion for suffering comes when, knowing right from wrong and being of clear mind, you choose to go against your better judgment.

Compared to such weighty questions as life and death, are you really going to be weighed down by things like the fear of getting canceled, of losing a friend, or even of your business failing?

Beware of those who offer to sell you an insurance policy against bad luck. Before you reach for your pen to sign up for such a policy, call to mind the words of the Dalai Lama:

> Remember that not getting what you want is
> sometimes a wonderful stroke of luck.

It may be that the superficially happy person is one whose luck has not yet turned. Better the one whose mettle has been tested and whose peace of mind has not been found wanting than one who has never had cause for complaint.

Fear of loss is just an emotion, and you are not your emotions. Even when your fears arise, in the stillness of your well-ordered mind, you can recognize them, observe them, and ignore them. Your fears will then lose their power over you and fade away.

The Bene Gesserit were the philosophers of Frank Herbert's Dune series. Whenever they felt their emotions rising, they chanted the Litany Against Fear:

> *I must not fear.*
> Fear is the mind-killer.
> Fear is the little-death that brings total obliteration.
> I will face my fear.
> I will permit it to pass over me and through me.
> And when it has gone past I will turn the inner eye to see its path.
> Where the fear has gone there will be nothing.
> Only I will remain.

I do not fear Greeks bearing gifts, at least when they come in this form, and today's gift comes courtesy of Epictetus:

> Men are disturbed, not by things, but by the principles and notions which they form concerning things. When therefore we are hindered, or disturbed, or grieved, let us never attribute it to others, but to ourselves.

We fear the loss of things because our fellow humans pursue them with such vigor. They would be devastated by losing their possessions, true, but that is no reason for you to lose your mind with worry.

Though a thousand tell you that wealth is the true measure of a person, and consequently, that loss of wealth is the worst that can happen, saying it does not make it so.

Fools do not make any more sense just because they are shouting.

Be well.

Chapter Six

On Admitting Mistakes

Now I ask you to ask yourself whether you can say you have never strayed from the path

R egarding the latest string of journalistic malfeasance at our favorite national newspaper, we must apply different treatments if we hope to effect a lasting cure.

The mistakes of the junior reporter are different than those of the senior editor. The first must be corralled gently but firmly back within the guidelines, while the latter requires a stiffer sentence.

We are no friends to our friends if we let misdeeds go unremarked. Leniency is appropriate only when the student appears to have learned their lesson.

"Why on earth" you ask, "do you think your message will penetrate the editor's head? The past several years have shown their slanted reporting is deliberate and no accident. Surely this one will acknowledge no mistake."

I may not be successful in my efforts, dear reader, but the only sure way to fail is not to try.

- Even though our patient seems too far gone for our medicine to bring relief, still we minister attention in the hope of recovery.

- For unlike terminal illnesses of the body, the mind may be regained no matter how far astray it has been led.

The reporter has already suffered from shaming and is open to guidance. The grooves of his mind are not so worn, such that the shock of public scorn will not move him.

So, because he is malleable, we shall shape his thinking in the direction of long-term value, not immediate gain. A shortcut to meet a deadline that cuts short your career is a poor bargain indeed.

The reporter has had his lesson reinforced and will walk the straight and narrow for now.

But I fear the temptation is only temporarily gone and not forgotten. The horse that once strays needs a tighter grip on the reins, for it has tasted the grass growing out of reach of those who follow the rules.

We may certainly redeem ourselves, but we bear watching until we prove again, if only to ourselves, that we are able to resist temptation.

Now I ask you to ask yourself whether you can say you have never strayed from the path.

- You are making progress in learning the things that are truly valuable, but you still value tangible things.

- Physical needs are slight, while wants know no limits.

- Wants multiply in your mind and the more you try to satisfy them, the more you burden your retinue with a train of baggage that stretches out behind you.

I will draw upon the account of the Buddha to enrich us with this saying:

> Empty the boat of your life, O man; when empty
> it will swiftly sail.

Leave behind all that does not lift you up, or you will be weighed down as surely as by any anchor.

When pointing out the flaws in others, it is all too easy to forget that we are not perfect ourselves. Thus, even as we are watching over our friends at the paper, you shall be an equally vigilant guard over your own thoughts.

You will allow me to stay in the Buddha's debt with this advice:

> Think not of the faults of others, of what they
> have done or not done. Think rather of your own
> sins, of the things you have done or not done.

Look first within.

Lest you think we profit today only from the Buddha's wisdom, take into your mental ownership this insight from A Father's Book of Wisdom:

> When you judge others, you are revealing your
> own fears and prejudices.

I have written to you before about the dangers of hypocrisy. I do not mean here just the dangers to your reputation, real enough though they are, but rather to yourself.

When you criticize another for something you do yourself, you are not only a false teacher, but a false student.

When you freely admit to your own mistakes, you render your opponents harmless. The best weapon is one you wield against yourself because this type of attack only makes you stronger.

Be well.

Chapter Seven

On Traveling to Change

What does it matter how many miles you put on your shoes if you do not first orient yourself in the desired direction?

Y ou are not the first person to be fooled by thinking that a change of place will lead to a change of heart.

Though you were told "A change is as good as a rest," your heart is heavy that you have not benefitted from changing jobs and changing house.

This is because you are looking for change in all the wrong places. If the lens through which you look at the world remains affixed to your eyes, is it any wonder you see the same things no matter how far you wander?

You may be the most minimalist of packers, needing nothing but a toothbrush and your ID, the Jack Reacher of philosophers. Still you are laden with that most weighty of baggage: yourself.

Pluck a small-minded person from Anywhere, USA, and place them down in a foreign land. Their prejudices will have made the trip without having paid a penny for the fare.

What does it matter how many miles you put on your shoes if you do not first orient yourself in the desired direction? You cannot outrun yourself. As Jon Kabat-Zinn put it in his book of the same name, "Wherever You Go, There You Are."

This is not as trivial as it sounds, so pause a moment and dwell on the thought and what it means to you.

If you do not know yourself at home, abroad you are but a stranger who also doesn't understand the local ways. Rather than easing your burdens, they become heavier with each step you travel, because now you are uncomfortable as well as confused.

When you carry a stranger within yourself, you will be bothered by strange food, strange smells, and strange faces.

When you are buffeted on all sides by a cacophony of voices, how likely is it you will listen to that small voice inside yourself? Some say it is the measure of success to be comfortable in discomfort and at ease when others are weary.

When you are learning to tame your mind, dear reader, you can be measured in the measures you take to test yourself.

A wise man does not subject himself to needless stress. Yes, we can overcome and thrive in any setting, but that does not mean we prefer to suffer. Put yourself at ease so that you may more easily confer with your inner thoughts.

You have time enough for displays of virtuosity when you have become master of yourself. I say be like those who have not traveled beyond their front porch but first explored the uncharted territory within.

Before I stop I will pay the toll for my fare today, and I will do so in the coin of Edith Schaeffer:

> People throw away what they could have by insisting on perfection, which they cannot have, and looking for it where they will never find it.

If you focus on your thoughts and motivations and values, you have a chance to earn peace of mind that no destination can afford you. The change that lies within you is one no change of place can deliver.

Be well.

Chapter Eight

On the Value of Work

The true value of work is when it brings you not possessions, but self-possession, and knowledge of what is worth pursuing and what can be safely cast aside

D ear reader, I see you clearly among the crowd. By your actions, you turn your potential into practice.

Keep along in this fashion, and you will be successful in the ways that matter most. You will learn self-knowledge and self-possession, and from these, you will know which things are to be valued and which are to be shunned.

Thus, will you have the elements for a happy life.

Your progress is under constant threat, not least when you are in the presence of other people. They will push you and pull you and exhort you to one course after another because that is the way of society.

The direction of travel does not matter so much as going along with the crowd, wherever it is headed. We can tolerate a foe in our midst more easily than a free thinker. The enemy's purpose and maneuvers we understand, while the independent-minded is unpredictable and subversive.

If you do not wish to be a traitor to your own thoughts, you must remove yourself from the presence of those constantly trying to influence them.

During the 40-day period of Lent, Christians live simply and give up luxuries so as to bring themselves closer to God.

The month of Ramadan for Muslims similarly calls upon the faithful to fast from all food and drink from dawn to sunset. It is not just the body, but also the mind, that is to be sharpened by this rigor: avoiding anger, envy, and other failings.

There is wisdom here, but also folly. If we are put on the path to virtue by relinquishing vices and reflecting on what is truly important, why would we tread that path for but a fraction of our time? Is a man wise who is sober on Monday and mindless the rest of the week?

No, dear reader, if you want to maintain your happiness more than momentarily, you must be the permanent master of your thoughts. Having painstakingly snared a cage full of sparrows, would you release them all only to start chasing them again the next day?

If you lapse, let it be because of an inadvertent slip rather than relaxing your grasp. Hold steady and hold fast to what you have gained. This is serious work and deserves your sincere attention.

The work of ordering your mind is worthwhile, but do not make the mistake of thinking that all work is equally worthy. Work itself is not its own reward.

We all know the aging executive haunting the office halls who says that without work they have no purpose. Without their title, their perks, and their pay, they would be cast adrift.

I say there is little purpose to such one's work. The ox labors mightily plowing one furrow after the other, but for all its exertions it neither knows nor cares in which direction it is pointed.

"How can I be sure" you ask, "if the work that I am doing is worthwhile?"

Only if you purposefully approach your work will your work have a purpose. The aim cannot be only money, or prestige, or power, although these may be by-products of your efforts. If such fruits of your labor come your way, by all means, enjoy them.

But you must guard yourself to ensure that to go without is no Lenten abstinence or Ramadan fast. Do not value a thing if possessing more of it brings you farther from contentment and peace.

Fortune gives and Fortune takes away, and it is not up to us to determine the portions we will receive.

You are not made better by your possessions, nor are you made less by lacking them. So why make yourself unhappy by wishing for what you do not have?

The true value of work is when it brings you not possessions, but self-possession, and knowledge of what is worth pursuing and what can be safely cast aside.

The wise farmer protects the freshly planted crops from predators and plows under the weeds. Each invasive plant you allow to take root will later steal water and light from your crop, reducing your yield. And even if one or two weeds will not overtake your field, remember that weeds grow unaided and multiply unseen.

Be well.

Chapter Nine

On Keeping Your Promise

It should give you pause to consider that the great many who think themselves in possession of their faculties are in fact being mindlessly swept along

Y ou have committed to living a good life. Having made the decision knowingly, you are now in a more precarious position than you were before.

You walk in full knowledge of the pitfalls that lay about you on all sides, and you cannot make those dangers disappear by closing your eyes to them.

Many will cast slings and arrows your way, saying things like "Go ahead, give up wants. Then you won't want to do anything but sit around all day like a lump!"

No, when you are about your business seriously, you can expect to be doubted and misunderstood and questioned without end.

Because you travel in your own measured way and do not keep pace with the many, those who notice you will try to bring you back to their rhythm, like a biker who has strayed from the peloton.

And when you say "Thank you, but no thanks," in reply "I have all I need," they will leave you for a fool.

"By all means," they'll cry, "rush to your death you seem to be so eager to prepare for."

It should give you pause to consider that the great many who think themselves in possession of their faculties are in fact being mindlessly swept along.

They are driven by the whip of desires and wants and emotions as surely as the drover plies his oxen. Onward they pull, carrying every burden behind them, because the only way they know is forward. But we know the only way to escape the yoke is to first realize that it lies upon our shoulders at all times, heavy and unyielding.

The key to unlocking ourselves from our burdens is for us to stop and think, though we are whipped in the resulting stillness by all we think we should be doing.

To go forward in the direction we were progressing is to make no progress. But take a turn ninety degrees in our minds and we can walk away from our shackles as if they had fallen to dust on our shoulders.

Once you know that at least some of your prisons are comprised entirely of your own mind and that you are your own jailor, you will be free to step outside the confines of your cell.

Thus, I say live up to your promise: You have your wits about you, and there is nothing more beneficial than living according to reason. You, having nothing, know that you have everything within yourself, and are content.

The witless are hopeless because they hope for what they have not.

Be well.

Chapter Ten

On Composure

Just as the glib speaker fools the lazy listener, so we mistake fervor in argument for conviction, and conviction for correctness

I t is a pleasure to receive your letters, though I repeat myself in saying it. I know that when you address me in this way, you are giving me your attention and more: You are giving me an insight into your mind, so that I may mark your progress.

A letter reveals much, and what has been written can no longer be hidden, from yourself or from your reader. And if I recognize in your words the unveiling of a fellow mind, it is because your letters bring to mind our conversations so well.

Don't fall in love with the sound of your own voice, dear reader. People who are facile with words risk remaining only superficial thinkers.

This is because they can talk their way around any obstacle, without regard to whether they have addressed the substance of their opponent's argument. They can dazzle and confuse with their eloquence, and because they are quick on their feet, the listener assumes they are correct in their conclusions.

But why should something done quickly be considered done well? Yes, efficiency and productivity deserve our praise, but not in all things.

And just as you can take an obsession over detail too far, so can you exaggerate in moving quickly. In what area of human endeavor do we praise the slapdash effort as the best one?

- Would you rather your painter spilled out color at great volume regardless of who or what gets splattered in the process?

- Or do you prefer the professional who carefully tapes off what they are working on and painstakingly addresses every detail?

Keep your wits about you, and let the wags rattle on. Just as the glib speaker fools the lazy listener, so we mistake fervor in argument for conviction, and conviction for correctness.

Shall we not be a little wary of the one who rages and foams at the mouth? Is their point made stronger by being delivered strongly? If we shower our audience in spittle, do we expect them to lean in for more, or to lean away?

Logorrhea of speaking or writing, with its diarrhea of words and repetition, is unpleasant to hear or read.

And it is not just unconvincing for all its volume. The more words you spill out, the more you will open yourself to criticism.

A carefully tended chain of thought has fewer but stronger links. An argument that stretches on for miles will be easily broken at many points, and so the whole of the journey may be called into question.

My core message is this: think long and speak short. Spend so much time in the company of your thoughts that you can deliver them briefly.

Be well.

Chapter Eleven

On Rumor and Fact

When we look at others, our views of reality are shaded by the tint of our own minds: our prejudices, our fears, and our faults

Y ou are wondering how I have found out what you were planning when you did not tell me yourself.

Nature offers up many seemingly inexhaustible resources: Water raining down to create lakes and oceans, fish to fill them, and sun and wind to keep the weather cycles streaming.

Another resource we will never run short of is rumors.

The tabloids at the checkout counter fill us in on the intimate details of the lives of the rich and famous. What would be trivial about any other, "He was spotted in Starbucks wearing an old sweater," is consumed avidly and questioned rarely.

We don't stop to question our prurient interest or our voyeuristic bent. So let me ask you, dear reader, why do you think we cannot look away?

I suspect one reason is this: People are poor at determining the value of something that stands alone, but we are savants when it comes to comparing two things.

Ask a person, "Do you like fruit?" and you will elicit a lukewarm "I guess, yes." Now ask them whether they prefer apples or bananas and you will hear them answer with confidence.

When it comes to celebrities, the tabloids hold them out to us not in splendid isolation, but as an implicit contrast to our own lives. "Look at their mansion, behold their supercar, bewonder their Caribbean vacation!"

These displays do not drive our admiration, but more often only discontent with our own lives.

We are much more likely to find bitterness, envy, and resentment when we peer over our neighbors' walls. The French have a proverb:

> What makes us discontented with our condition
> is the absurdly exaggerated idea we have of the
> happiness of others.

We see the outward signs of others' success, and we forget both the sacrifices that were demanded and the inner struggles that remain.

When we look at others, our views of reality are shaded by the tint of our own minds: Our prejudices, our fears, and our faults.

The rumor we read on the page or concoct in our heads is never reflective of reality. So why do we collect and pass on rumors, like couriers supplying narcotics to their addicted clientele?

It is because we know a scandal or fall from grace is never far. Rumors bite, they bleed. They tell us that our life cannot be so bad, because look how badly that one screwed theirs up.

This is a comparison we gladly make. It is the promise of a boost that comes from another's fall that keeps us coming back to the water cooler. But it is no noble thing to delight in another's misery.

To not feel elevated by another's fall is the first step in understanding that your worth is measured only by your own thoughts and deeds.

Focus on the facts of your own actions and give rumors no run of your thoughts.

Be well.

Chapter Twelve

On Role Models

Those who see much while believing they know little are much rarer and more valuable than those who believe they know much and consequently see little

L ike hikers caught in a sudden snowstorm, dear reader, we are easily led off the path we wish to follow.

Despite our strenuous effort and determined gait, we can find ourselves after a lengthy march only to have wandered in a great circle and ending up back where we started.

When it comes to matters of desire versus reason, wishful thinking is no guide at all. What we need is the philosophical equivalent of a satellite high up in space, untouchable yet reaching out to us with a steady signal to remind us at all times not only of our current position but our heading and speed as well.

Where are we to find such GPS guides for the soul?

Consider first whether the truth of a proposition depends on who is propounding it. This is not as easy to see through as it seems, so let's spend some moments here before we move on.

At one extreme we have acknowledged experts, which is to say people who have devoted serious time and attention to a topic. You will identify them by their credentials and degrees.

Surely, we should grant the expert the greatest degree of credibility? I am reminded of what Napoleon supposedly said about the practice of law, namely that it sharpens the mind by making it narrow.

Those who see everything through a single lens miss all that is outside their immediate gaze. It is when you are in the midst of the most credible, dear reader, that you should most hold fast to your credulity.

Experts are among the easiest to fool, not least when they are fooling themselves in pursuit of publishing. Thus forewarned, you will more clearly see the signs of their folly, which are to be found in the fact that they are either speaking or writing.

At the other end of this uneven seesaw, we find the great mass of humanity. I do not doubt that many have the talent and ability to uncover truths if they would but put in the effort.

Alas, the easiest road to travel is the one that leads down the path of least resistance.

So not having the inclination to study a subject deeply themselves, they incline to the best available proxy: What does everyone else think? If we can find it on the front pages of the New York Times or the Washington Post, why should we tax ourselves to travel a step further?

The absolute truth of a matter is irrelevant if everyone in your neighborhood believes the opposite.

This is how we find supposedly serious people debating which way the weight of consensus opinion tips. As if such light things as opinions could be tallied up to create something of substance!

A googol of zeros does not add up to more than one hundred ones multiplied by one another. And yet a single dissenting voice can reveal a previously unseen flaw that renders entire foundations of science unstable.

Who are these few who can, with a word, end the debate? Or if they do not bring it to its terminus, who can shift the train of discussion in an entirely new direction?

The truly wise do not come in common guise, dear reader, although we can call forth some common properties among them. One who sees much and says little is more likely to scatter treasures after them than trifles.

The Buddha identifies their opposite number when he reminds us:

One is not wise because one speaks much.

Those who see much while believing they know little are much rarer and more valuable than those who believe they know much and consequently see little.

In "*The Art of War*," Sun Tzu describes the clever fighter as one who not only wins, but excels in winning with ease. Hence his victories bring him neither reputation for wisdom nor credit for his courage.

If you have clawed back from the brink through mighty effort, but it was your own actions that placed you first in peril, why should we celebrate your heroics?

If you agonize over every choice and second-guess yourself the moment you decide, are you a better arbiter than the one who silently chooses the correct path and simply implements it?

The most virtuous role models are not calling out to lead. They do not call out at all, because they do not believe their right to speak outweighs any other's.

You will see their handiwork in their actions, not their proclamations. They know that they are no farther than a single step from a fall, so do not claim to be perfect. This, even though you never see them place a false step.

"But you still have not told me" you cry, "where and how to find these gurus. If they are not among the ranks of experts, nor to be found among the bestsellers list, where should I turn to for guidance?"

I have two suggestions, dear reader, and you will not be surprised at the first, which is to look within.

All that is good (and not coincidentally all that is bad), is discerned by your reason. You are your own most trusted guru, for none knows you better.

If you slow down enough to query the truth of your honest heart and your well-ordered mind, you will know the wisdom of your actions before you lift a finger.

But we rush to action without thought when we should be rushing to pass judgment on our actions.

If you must look without, then look to that which has passed the test of time. I don't mean what passes for consensus opinion, but rather that which bears up under the weight of the ages.

Human nature bedeviled our ancient forebears as much as it bedevils us now. And because they had both great tribulations and few distractions, our ancestors busied themselves with the enduring questions of what it means to live a good life in accordance with one's nature and reason.

And if we find ourselves still returning to their answers more than 2,000 years later, the chances are good they gave good answers.

Again, I caution you not to be misled by a name.

- As much as Seneca illuminates, he sometimes sheds light where it does not help us.

- As poignant as Marcus Aurelius' meditations are, he was reminding himself of some things that we do not need repeated.

- And even the sayings of Confucius and the Buddha are but map and guidepost, not the territory itself.

Study the greats carefully so that you can imagine them standing before you when you are contemplating your own actions.

Look to them as role models, not for what they say, but for how they would act.

Be well.

Chapter Thirteen

On Calm Amidst Bedlam

To retire from work life does not mean you have retired from your worries. To take the one step without taking the other is to change places but not position

The well-ordered mind in relaxation provides deep tranquility. Can it be achieved in conditions of disturbance?

I wrote you that I traveled to New York, and I fear I exaggerated the petty insults of the journey to make my point.

My tests were not passed upon my arrival, dear reader. For my hotel was directly on Times Square, and I will not say who recommended this as a good idea. Perhaps they thought I wanted to be close to all that New York has to offer and, if so, they know me not.

The only proximity I sought was to my own thoughts, though this is what was in fact near to me in my cell above Broadway and 43rd Street:

- a constant background din that must be experienced to be believed, consisting of a byzantine blend of taxis honking their horns;

- delivery trucks' rumbling diesel engines, slamming doors, and metal grating of ramps being slid across rear cargo beds;

- the piercing "BEEP! BEEP! BEEP!" of reversing construction equipment;

- garbagemen banging trash tubs into their trucks' crushing metal embrace;

- police whistles seeking attention and directing traffic;

- storeowners heaving skyward the heavy mesh gates protecting their precious wares; and

- the hucksters and tourists in their simultaneously hopeful and skeptical commerce.

The noise presses in from all sides:

- the thump of suspiciously heavy things dropped on the floor above me, the proverbial penny and other shoe making repeat appearances;

- the inanities of CNN blaring through the walls on one side of me, and the conspiracies of FOX on the other;

- drunken voices now shouting, laughing, and

stumbling their way down the hallway;

- hotel doors slamming shut with the solidity of stone tomb lids; and

- helicopters whirling overhead to ferry the prominent to their Hamptons estates.

You observe blackout curtains upon entering your room, and you wonder if this is some paranoid preparation for keeping night lights hidden in wartime.

A glance out the window reveals the reason, for you are as well-served here wearing sunglasses at midnight as at noon.

I wouldn't wonder to learn that neon is no longer naturally occurring, for it seems to have been transported *en masse* into tubes lining every surface of every building around Times Square. If aliens in space nearing our planet need a beacon to guide them on, New Yorkers need but continue to pay their electricity bills.

The only relief from the brilliant flickering glare comes when great gouts of steam rise from vents and tubes piercing the cracked streets like Hell's own ventilation system.

Lest I overdo my dramatization once again, let me tell you, dear reader, that none of this bedlam affected me in the slightest.

When I am deep in my reading or writing, I retreat into a world inside my mind and the outside fades from my senses. Those blaring notes which would deafen another I scarcely note.

In this state, my well-ordered mind keeps me focused within, and external distractions have no power over me.

In contrast, without the practice of calming the mind, you could sink a person in a deep-sea submersible to the bottom of the Mariana Trench where no light or sound or sensation intrude, and yet they would be bothered.

We carry our troubles with us and can raise ourselves to states of excitement wholly out of proportion to any external instigation.

Though the decibel meter shows absolute silence, still the troubled hear the voices of arguments raging inside them, the pitiful cries of regret, and the insatiable calling out for more.

I have urged you to hold fast to your plans to retire from your post, dear reader, and to join me in retreat from professional pursuits.

To retire from work life does not mean you have retired from your worries. To take the one step without taking the other is to change places but not position.

If you are successful in letting reason order your mind you have no reason to be discomfited by all the noise and bustle that accosts you, whether it be from opinions of the ignorant, from praise or blame from any source, or from being in the busiest of cities.

Whisk a wise person into the center of Shanghai, Mumbai, or Mexico City, or into the center of a maelstrom of argument whipped by heated emotions, and they will be as at peace as in a mountainous meditation retreat.

Though we test ourselves periodically to ensure we are up to the task, we should not live permanently in the madhouse to prove we are sane.

I am just as happy to walk easily as I am to make my way uphill, and I do not seek out the treacherous path if I can easily detour past it.

Thus, I will soon depart from this bedlam and would that more people understand that the door is unlocked, and they too are free to walk away from their personal prisons!

Be well.

Chapter Fourteen

On Outrunning Yourself

Rather than looking to travel in more luxury and greater style, we should sit still with ourselves and consider whether we are running to something or running away from it

D eparture day and I am on the road again!

I aim always to be a sincere student, dear reader, and this means learning the lessons from my trials. Hence it was that I made my way by foot from the doors of my Times Square hotel and down the broad sidewalks flanking Broadway.

No taxi to lure me in like a Venus flytrap only to hold me immobile and despairing of escape. I walk on past the stairways leading into the steamy depths of the subway, for there is nowhere they can transport me I want to go.

And none of JKF, LaGuardia, or Newark will tempt me today only to leave me sitting. For there are only waiting gates and delayed gates, but no departure gates.

"How then" you ask, "did you plan to make your escape from the city, if you were avoiding all these means of transport?"

Ah, my clever plan was this: Take to my own two feet, which have never failed me. I journeyed south down Seventh, west on 42nd, and there avoided the first shoals of my journey.

The Port Authority Bus Terminal was not my plan, for I was seeking to make my escape from madness, and not to become mired in the quicksand of lost souls.

Safely past to the corner of Eighth, and I strode on down to Penn Station. The iron rails were my last refuge, dear reader, a hitherto reliable link to the state capitol, where Albany's little airport beckoned.

Though I am unwillingly online, I knew enough from prior journeys to both order my ticket in advance on Amtrack.com and to reserve a seat on the grandly named Empire Service.

Past the lingering lines of the lost snaking their way to ticket windows, the self-service kiosk cheerfully spits out my ticket with no more than a passing greeting from my credit card.

Oh, to see the great hall of Penn Station, where travelers direct their gazes up to the screens overhead, eagerly awaiting announcement of their track.

- Don't watch the people, play with your cell phone, or let your attention wander.

- Suddenly a group takes off at a sprint, dragging

    suitcases and clutching loose bags to their side, their number has been called!

- If you have positioned yourself at the wrong end of the station, if you hesitate, you are left behind.

Past trips have left the bitter taste of experience in my mouth, for I know that though the Empire Service may originate on a different track each time, the line for boarding always forms in the same place.

On the side of the great hall, in sniffing distance of the Dunkin Donuts if not quite close enough to touch, you must wait. Line up an hour before your train is to depart, and you will not be too early.

Book in hand, your hour flies by, and you are on the train moments after the boarding has begun. Locate your seat, tend to your bags.

Then begins my favorite part of the journey: The first half hour as the train haltingly navigates the secret underground corridors of New York and emerges into the wide-open Hudson Valley.

The lights on the train flicker on and off as the train shunts from track to track. Is the train supposed to lurch from side to side that much?

Periodically you hear the static of a conductor's announcement, the crackle a hint that something is being said, but I have never deciphered a single word.

In those moments when the train is dark and you are still underground, sometimes a beam of light thrusts in from an improbable angle above, lighting up fantastic and ever-changing manmade landscapes.

Graffiti, of course. I cannot look away. I will not be surprised if the first sign of non-human intelligent life we find is a graffiti tag left behind by a bored alien teenager at the base of a red cliff on Mars.

Then there are the detritus of human existence, some expected, like bottles and cans, filthy blankets, paper scraps blown in from the streets above, a mattress, rats, both living and not, but other things so unexpected that you marvel at what extremity brought them to these places: The shopping cart at least has wheels, I guess someone could have wheeled it there, but the refrigerator, the set of dining chairs?

Though your eyes strain in the dark, and you almost imagine you saw a shadow receding into the corner, I have never seen the citizens who must make their homes here or at least pass some time among the dusty cinders.

How do they access these realms, and how again do they alight? And what do they think when they see the lit windows of the Amtrack car? The faces of all within reflecting the blue glow of their phones and tablets, for am I the only one looking out?

I think the reason people so readily focus on outward appearances, dear reader, is that they are afraid to look within.

When I tell you that the worth of a person is not to be found in the clothes draped on their shoulders, or the car they adorn themselves with, think for a moment how hard we two work to ensure reason holds pride of place in our minds. Think how much toil is required to achieve this ease.

Many all too willingly embrace the external to avoid facing the internal. For how many would find within themselves well-ordered and well-lit rooms instead of scattered debris, cast-off possessions, and wild-haired inhabitants lurking in dark corners?

Though we travel to the ends of the earth, we cannot outrun ourselves.

Rather than looking to travel in more luxury and greater style, we should sit still with ourselves and consider whether we are running to something or running away from it.

If we work to clear away the weeds from a portion of our mind and carefully pick up and discard the broken glass of poor decisions in our past, we may create a place of rest and calm within us that we can retreat to at will.

Be well.

Chapter Fifteen

On Joy and Enjoyment

Joy as we understand it does not depend on what possessions you are currently enjoying, and what pleasurable experiences you may be seeking

I enjoyed reading your latest commentary. I say enjoyment in the usual meaning of the term, dear reader, and not the philosophical mean we aim for.

Enjoyment is what one commonly feels when the way is easy, and distractions are few. I would normally tell you that enjoyment is no sign of virtue, but rather of an uncontrolled mind.

For most, enjoyment is the condition that signals its opposite is not far behind, and is thus not to be confused with joy, which when attained is lasting.

Joy as we understand it does not depend on what possessions you are currently enjoying, and what pleasurable experiences you may be seeking. It is a condition arising from a tranquil mind, undisturbed by external things.

You may take enjoyment in your friend's business success, her new house, and her doting spouse, but when we remember that all of these are potential fault lines from which future disappointment may yawn wide, we will not mistake the feeling for joy, which cannot be undone by any reversal of fortune.

I did take pleasure from your commentary, and I will tell you why I enjoyed it.

You put words into service with purpose and meaning, and your army of words is both varied and wide. The rich vocabulary you call into the field is employed to illuminate and not obfuscate.

I am compelled to pay attention, but I do so eagerly because I am not kept long waiting for a tangible example to illustrate an ephemeral point.

Sometimes I am rewarded with a simile, like when you compared the author's writing to orderly rows of corn in the field, stretching uniformly into the distance.

Sometimes it is a metaphor, for example, calling wealth a weight that pins us down to places and pursuits that hold us captive more than they free us.

If I can draw an analogy, the evidence of your clear thinking can be found in your clear writing, just as a pure source of water will generate a clear stream even though it travels over a muddy bed.

I will not go on in this vein, because I am mindful of what Confucius once said of his student:

> Hui does not help me — he takes such delight in
> everything I say.

I would help you, and not just praise you, so I will tell you what else Confucius brings to mind on this topic. It is that wisdom bubbles up from many sources, and these springs flow freely for us all.

If you want confirmation that we are but keepers of the waters of wisdom rather than its possessors, consider this: The Roman philosophers we are so fond of reading were performing their mental gymnastics some 2,000 years ago, and they made frequent reference to the "ancients" that were their inspiration, including the Greek thinkers that pre-dated them by half a millennium.

In the East, Confucius lived and died 500 years before Cicero walked the earth, yet Confucius looked to the principles of the Zhou religion that were ancient in his day.

Considering the pace of technological change, the year 2500 is as far from us today as we are from the Roman Stoics.

Should we doubt that those who follow in the centuries long after we are dead and gone will look back upon our "modern times" and consider our practices and our troubles ancient?

But the wisdom we lay claim to is not ours, it is the common property of humankind.

When we look back into the deep recesses of time and compare what our forebears had to bear, many people living today have every reason to be masters of themselves, for they have been given rich advantages:

- a lifespan that is three times as long as what humans enjoyed even two hundred years ago, and one that is marked by remarkable health and curing of disease;

- societies freely organized under principles of individual freedom and inalienable rights;

- the accountability and certainty arising from the rule of law, with life, liberty, and property coming under the protection of the state.

When the ancients talked of freeing themselves from the burdens of fortune, their concerns included

- imprisonment, banishment, war, slavery, torture, and death, to name but a few. Not only their own deaths, but those of their children, siblings, partners, and friends;

- reversals of fortune that would keep Hollywood scriptwriters salivating for years;

- the rise and fall of empires!

In our absolute comfort and ease, with ready access to all the world's wisdom, and with the least to objectively complain of, we are among the unhappiest of all generations.

How to explain the riddle that for all our enjoyment, joy consistently eludes us?

In being surrounded by plenty we have not grown virtuous but have grown accustomed to vice. Our enjoyment of easy pleasures has made us flabby of mind, as undisciplined as a college wrestler gone to fat in middle age, maintaining bulk while losing substance.

Used to having everything at our fingertips, no more than a one-click order and same-day delivery away, we no longer appreciate what we have.

When your freedom and your very life are forfeit to the whims of chance, you cannot help but think about what things are of real value. When you not only cannot control your own suffering, but you see it meted out with a generous hand all around you, you appreciate fully when you are not suffering.

The ancients faced mighty troubles and found ways to nonetheless not be troubled.

The purpose of holding troubles in your mind, dear reader, is not to be consequently plagued by worry about what might happen or not happen. You become the thief of your own peace of mind when you worry about others taking it from you.

Think on troubles to remind yourself that these are troubles only in your thoughts and hold no power over your mind. You will achieve lasting joy by remembering that while it may be found in enjoyment, enjoyment is not its exclusive domain.

When you are free from doubt, worry, and jealousy; when your course is the same whether you are pushing into the headwind or blown along by a tailwind; when you delight in stillness as much as you do in motion; when you do not rely on external things, joy is your reward.

Be well.

Chapter Sixteen

On Endurance

Virtue lies not in hard circumstances themselves, but in being able to endure hardships without upset or complaint

I am just returned from a run through the forest paths and farmer's fields near my home.

In springtime I run the risk of encountering every condition when I step out my door: Though the sun is peeking out behind clouds when I set out, I may be confronted with a sudden squall of rain, by hail if I am unlucky, and wind that whips the treetops, not to mention my bare legs.

This time I was blessed with all that nature has to offer, with the result that I got first overheated, then soaked, then chilled.

I now warm myself with the prospect of a pleasant conversation with you, dear reader. Not a heated one, but one in which I can bask in the reflected glow of a point well-made, and a connection made between minds.

Judging from your questions about my recent letter, I cannot take my rest yet, but will put my efforts to explaining one particular topic that seems to be bothering you.

For you ask, "If the first-order and second-order pursuits are equally valuable, that means they are equally desirable. And if they are desirable, that means I should seek them out. But how does it make sense for me to welcome the ill-winds of conflict, to court obstacles, or to look for ill-health?"

I have learned physical endurance from my running training, and you have learned endurance of another kind reading my letters: Patience with me getting to my point. So let me get straight to the substance here.

Just like the courts draw a distinction between murder and manslaughter, though the victim is just as dead in both cases, so must you draw a distinction between these different circumstances, dear reader.

The state of mind is the key, your intentions are everything. Virtue lies not in hard circumstances themselves, but in being able to endure hardships without upset or complaint.

When you let reason rule your mind you will not prefer a fight, but you will address it head-on when it cannot be avoided.

- You will not knowingly or unnecessarily make your path more difficult, nor will you complain about the obstacles you inevitably encounter.

- You do not welcome the fever you feel accompanying a cough, but you also do not recoil in terror at the thought of what you may have caught.

Imagine what a world it would be if we could only find value in things that were pleasant and easy! How many would suffer without end, because it is the fate of many to be without pleasant and easy times.

There is virtue in rising to your circumstances, whatever they may be. The things you work the hardest for are consequently easiest to see the value in.

Meet your challenges openly, calmly, with reason ruling your passions, and you will be rewarded with a well-ordered mind that brings peace, no matter the chaos you find yourself in.

I reward your attention today by stopping, lest I run on in this letter like I have done before.

Be well.

Chapter Seventeen

On Adversity

The only misfortune you need to focus on is the fact that you feel the need to resist and complain

After all we have discussed, I see you are resisting and complaining about the misfortunes that have befallen you.

Have you not learned the lesson, or have you forgotten, that the only misfortune you need to focus on is the fact that you *feel the need* to resist and complain? There is no sadness for people in existence unless they find something in the world they think is sad.

- I am weary from work and my body is becoming frail; that is my fate and the fate of all people.

- None of the cryptocurrencies I buy are promoted by Elon Musk, my blog had just three visitors last month, and I have forgotten more passwords than I can remember.

- On all sides, I am beset by selfish neighbors, ungrateful employees, and greedy customers.

None of this daunts me. The default state of existence is hardship, not ease. I tell myself this not only to learn to *accept* the nature of life but to *expect* it.

I will not be surprised by the adversity that comes my way. On the contrary, I welcome having revealed to me each day what difficulty I must now overcome. I greet my obstacles with relish and a ready smile.

I understand your dismay, dear reader.

Between the lines of your anxious letters, I read your worry about your sudden insomnia and hair loss. Here now, I will say what you could not. You dread that you have some form of cancer, as if by not saying the word you can keep it from finding its way to your door.

The longer one lives, having survived all the outrages and accidents that carry off the young, the more likely one is to fall prey to an ailment from within. Replication errors within your DNA multiply exponentially as you multiply your years and expose your cells to ever more free radicals.

Are you not supremely greedy to wish that you alone can be made exempt from the laws of nature?

It is human nature to suffer and to struggle. I say open your eyes fully and accept the reality that surrounds us.

Embrace the battle and become master of your fate, not subject to it. Face adversity head on and you will be the hero of your own life, and there is no better way to live your life.

Thus you will understand me when I wish you all the best by wishing you a life not free from adversity, but full of clarity.

Be well.

Chapter Eighteen

On Self-Care

There is no distance we should not travel to find a cure for what ails us. But I would have you reflect that no amount of travel will help us if we are treating the wrong illness

O ver the centuries, we have tried many ways to cure the ailments that afflict humankind.

Before we understood antibiotics, the sanatorium was the preferred course of treatment for tuberculosis. Patients were sent off to new facilities in the hopes that fresh air and good nutrition would cure them.

There was money to be made from the treatment, never mind the cure, and so people experimented with many different methods.

- Altitude and cold mountain air became the approach for Switzerland; in Finland, it was remote forests that offered the best environment.

- In the western United States, we tried a mix of scenery and a lack of stress in North Carolina and later deemed the dry desert air of Arizona best at effecting a cure.

- Long after the lake air of the East Coast was tried, the ocean breezes of the West Coast emerged as front runners for convalescents.

For much longer than we shipped off the ailing on their healing journeys, the healthy made pilgrimages in the name of wellness.

- We have tried hot springs and spas, with volcanically heated pools and minerally infused waters.

- We heated saunas to steam us like so much slow-roasted pork.

- Then there are those who take the opposite plunge, submersing themselves in glacial waters so cold it snatches your breath away.

- Or consider mud wraps, salt scrubs, and seaweed masks. All the things we would normally wash away with alacrity if we fell into them by accident, we now pay great sums to have slathered on our bodies.

- Pedicure, manicure, massage; massage in every variation: Hot stone, deep tissue, full body, Swedish, sports, Shiatsu. Who knew there were so many ways to bring a recalcitrant muscle back in line?

Lest you take my list for a complaint, dear reader, let me make clear I do not object to self-care. Self-care is critical for well-being.

There is no distance we should not travel to find a cure for what ails us. But I would have you reflect that no amount of travel will help us if we are treating the wrong illness.

Some of us have serious physical ailments, it is true, but we all have mental afflictions. And these are not cured by our spa pilgrimage, no matter how expensive it may be. To effect a cure of our mental ills we must first journey within our minds to identify the sickness.

The most common cause of mental stress is to place the wrong value on external things.

The many who think wealth is a worthy pursuit are plagued by not having attained it. No matter how much they amass, they are goaded on by the fear of it never being enough and by envy of those who have still more than they do.

We all know a person who makes themselves ill with stress and a hypochondriac who in worrying about becoming ill actually accomplishes the feat that nature did not.

Before you take in the water, the air, or the scenery of a new destination, take a moment to consider the value you place on things. Take instruction from the great philosophers before you take the physician's cure.

Rather than having your muscles pulled this way and that, pull yourself out of your comfortable, unquestioning existence. You do not need to travel to resorts or spend money in spas to realize that your satisfaction does not come from the outside.

You are most pleased with yourself not when everything goes easily but when you have encountered and overcome obstacles and met your challenges head-on.

The hard way is hard, but along that path lies satisfaction and peace. And in any event, you cannot avoid the hard path in life, so are well-advised to embrace it when it comes even if you do not seek it out.

The easy path only seems easy, because going down this road leaves us flabby and unfulfilled, unprepared for the slightest setback. If we can only be happy when everything continues to be perfect, we are living a precarious existence indeed.

Knowing that hardship is part of what it means to be human, we take better care of ourselves when we are prepared for adversity. We prepare by contemplating the lessons of philosophy.

Though this commitment is also a cost we must pay, unlike the bill at the spa the investment in philosophy pays dividends our whole lives long.

Be well.

Chapter Nineteen

On Accepting the Inevitable

Think about the possibility of a hundred hardships. Better yet, expect them to afflict you at any moment

I can scarcely believe my ears to hear you carrying on so, dear reader. Have you forgotten everything we have been discussing? Does it take no more than an inconvenience to throw you off course and set you back to the beginning of your studies?

Three of your employees have given notice that they are leaving for greener pastures. That is their perfect right, or have you in your delusional state also forgotten that you work with paid employees and not Roman slaves?

If you paused in your lamentations to examine your thoughts, you would realize the true cause of your anguish.

- You are put to some inconvenience because you must now conduct a replacement search, and not just one but three! This takes time and is certainly a distraction from the daily business.

- Worse, you are worried about what your colleagues may think of you. Will they consider these defections a reflection of your leadership?

- But I think most of all, you are secretly worried that your former employees are giving not just two weeks' notice to the company, but giving *you* notice of some defect in you yourself.

I can almost hear you wondering whether the old saying is true "Employees don't leave companies, they leave bosses."

Recognize these thoughts for the signs of weakness that they are, dear reader, and give them no leave to plague your mind. You will no doubt spend some time finding your new teammates but think about what opportunities this gives you to upgrade your team.

I have taught myself to find the positive in every situation, for this is a habit you can practice like any other. If you have yet to find the upside, assume it is because you are not looking in the right place and keep looking.

Your colleagues may think ill of you. What of it? You know as well as I do that people project onto others their own fears and desires. If they are prone to assume that your employee turnover signals trouble, then you may entertain the thought that they have their own troubles to deal with.

And as to your self-doubt, this is one condition that you can bring about and multiply merely by thinking of it.

Remember instead that all feedback is useful to you, either revealing something of the giver or something about you. In either case, make it your own and use it to better yourself. If the feedback is from a trusted source and true, you now have a profitable topic to pursue. And otherwise, the input should be easy to dismiss.

Epictetus provides a helpful summary of the point I would have you take from this discussion. Perhaps his words will resonate with you if mine have not:

> Some things are in our control and others not. Things in our control are opinion, pursuit, desire, aversion, and, in a word, whatever are our own actions. Things not in our control are body, property, reputation, command, and, in one word, whatever are not our own actions.

The broader point I would make is this: Ask yourself in all situations, do you improve your position by complaining? This typically only serves to magnify minor complaints into larger ones.

And even if your misfortune is truly major — the death of a close friend, failure of your business, or a diagnosis of serious illness — will you make it worse by losing your well-ordered mind and railing against fate? What is the benefit of making yourself unhappy and irrational because the things that are destined to happen to humankind in fact happen?

"But they are not destined to happen to me!" goes the reply. "*Others* will get ill and die and suffer bad luck. I expected *my life* to be charmed at all turns."

This is no more than a pleasant fantasy, a daydream for children. Do you complain that the world is unfair? That you have not been allotted the same portion of good luck as some other, imaginary person? You would be as justified to complain that the sun rises each morning to disturb your sleep, that ants invade your picnic, or that your lottery numbers never get called.

Though fairness in life is unevenly distributed, there is one thing that we all share alike: Our mortality. We are each destined to die.

If you wish to feel better about the unfairness of it all, consider that the luckiest, wealthiest, and most beautiful people are all going to die. They are going to leave their charmed lives behind all the more grudgingly compared with those who have endured hardship and defeat. Tell me, will their deaths be any less final than your own?

You should not become spiteful in considering the fate that awaits all humankind. Nor should you become fearful at the thought of the misfortunes that may befall you.

By thinking about all the things that can happen to you, you prepare yourself to deal with them appropriately. The fact that bad news comes as a surprise is often all that is necessary to throw your reason temporarily out of balance. It can come as no surprise to one who has contemplated misfortune in advance.

Think about the possibility of a hundred hardships. Better yet, expect them to afflict you at any moment. Not only will you be ready for whatever comes your way, you will say "Is this all? I expected much worse."

The same situation, happening to the same person, but the reaction makes all the difference. If contemplating misfortune is part of the cure from misery when ill winds blow, are you better off dreaming only of pleasant things?

I leave you with the words of American theologian Reinhold Niebuhr, who also manages to summarize my point in far fewer words with his aptly named serenity prayer:

> God, grant me the serenity to accept the things I cannot change,
> courage to change the things I can,
> and wisdom to know the difference.

Be well.

9 7 8 1 9 6 8 7 2 3 2 2 4